AI Unplugged: Navigating the Good, the Bad, and the Future.

YAW BOATENG

Table of Contents

Chapter 1: Introduction to AI

Understanding Artificial Intelligence

Artificial Intelligence (AI) has emerged as a transformative force in various aspects of our lives, shaping industries, enhancing daily activities, and raising profound ethical questions. At its core, AI refers to the simulation of human intelligence processes by machines, particularly computer systems. These processes include learning from data, reasoning, problem-solving, and understanding natural language. This technology encompasses various subfields, such as machine learning, where algorithms improve through experience, and natural language processing, which allows machines to comprehend and generate human language. Understanding AI is crucial, as it not only informs discussions about its implications but also empowers individuals to engage with the technology more critically.

AI's impact is felt across diverse sectors, including healthcare, education, and environmental sustainability. In healthcare, for instance, AI algorithms can analyze extensive medical data to assist in diagnosing diseases and predicting patient outcomes. This capability not only enhances the quality of patient care but also streamlines operations within healthcare facilities. In education, AI-driven tools personalize learning experiences, catering to individual student needs and helping educators identify areas where students may require additional support. As these advancements continue, they underscore the potential of AI to improve efficiency and effectiveness in critical areas of society.

However, the rise of AI is not without challenges and ethical concerns. One of the most pressing issues is job displacement, as automation threatens to replace human workers in various industries. While AI can create new job opportunities, particularly in tech and data analysis fields, there is a growing concern about the skills gap that may leave many workers behind. Addressing these challenges requires a collaborative approach involving policymakers, educators, and industry leaders to ensure that workers are equipped with the necessary skills for a rapidly changing job market.

Furthermore, the ethical implications of AI cannot be overlooked. Bias in AI algorithms is a significant concern, as these systems can inadvertently perpetuate existing societal inequalities. The data used to train AI models often reflects historical biases, leading to skewed outcomes in applications such as hiring practices and law enforcement. Recognizing and mitigating these biases is essential for the responsible development and deployment of AI technologies. Continued dialogue about ethical standards and regulatory frameworks will be crucial in navigating the complexities of AI's integration into society.

As we look to the future, the role of AI in creative industries, national security, and environmental sustainability will likely expand. From enhancing artistic expression to improving security measures, AI's potential is vast. However, this also raises questions about creativity, authorship, and privacy. Balancing innovation with ethical considerations will be key to harnessing the benefits of AI while minimizing its risks. The ongoing evolution of AI necessitates a proactive approach to understanding its capabilities, challenges, and implications, ensuring that society can benefit from this powerful technology while safeguarding fundamental rights and values.

Historical Overview of AI Development

The development of artificial intelligence has been a gradual journey, marked by key milestones that reflect both technological advancement and evolving societal perceptions. The origins of AI can be traced back to the mid-20th century, when pioneers like Alan Turing and John McCarthy began to explore the concept of machines simulating human intelligence. Turing's seminal paper, "Computing Machinery and Intelligence," posed the provocative question, "Can machines think?"

This inquiry laid the groundwork for future AI research, fostering a vision of intelligent systems capable of performing tasks that typically require human cognitive functions.

In the following decades, AI experienced periods of optimism and disillusionment known as "AI winters," during which funding and interest dwindled due to unmet expectations. Early successes in narrow AI, such as game-playing programs and simple problem-solving tasks, contrasted sharply with the complexity of human reasoning and understanding. The challenges of natural language processing and machine learning techniques became apparent, yet researchers persevered, gradually developing more sophisticated algorithms. The resurgence of interest in AI in the 21st century can be attributed to advancements in computational power, the availability of vast amounts of data, and breakthroughs in machine learning, particularly deep learning.

The ethical implications of AI have come to the forefront of discussions as its applications have expanded into various sectors, including healthcare, education, and environmental sustainability. The ability of AI to analyze large datasets has revolutionized diagnostic tools, personalized learning experiences, and even strategies for combating climate change. However, these advancements also raise critical questions about accountability, transparency, and the potential for bias within AI systems. As AI becomes increasingly integrated into daily life, the ethical considerations surrounding its use require careful examination and proactive engagement from both developers and society at large.

As AI technologies continue to evolve, so too do concerns about job displacement and its impact on the workforce. Automation has the potential to streamline operations and enhance productivity, yet it also poses challenges for workers in industries susceptible to technological disruption. While some jobs may vanish, new opportunities will emerge, requiring a reevaluation of skills and education. The dialogue around AI's role in the workforce emphasizes the importance of preparing for a future where humans and machines collaborate, highlighting the need for policies that promote workforce adaptability and continuous learning.

4

Looking ahead, the future of AI holds immense possibilities, but it also demands careful consideration of regulatory frameworks to guide its development and use. Governments and organizations must strike a balance between fostering innovation and ensuring that AI technologies align with societal values and ethical standards. By addressing biases in algorithms, safeguarding personal privacy, and ensuring equitable access to AI benefits, stakeholders can work towards a future where AI enhances human potential while minimizing risks. This historical overview serves as a foundation for understanding the complexities and nuances of AI's evolution, shaping the discourse around its implications for society.

The Current Landscape of AI Technology

The current landscape of AI technology is marked by rapid advancements and a growing integration into various aspects of daily life. From personal assistants like Siri and Alexa to complex systems used in healthcare and finance, AI is reshaping how we interact with technology. These developments are not only enhancing efficiency but also raising important questions about ethics, privacy, and the implications of machine learning on jobs and social structures. As AI continues to evolve, understanding its capabilities and limitations becomes crucial for the general public and those engaged in specific niches.

One of the most significant areas of AI development is its application in healthcare. AI technologies are being utilized to analyze medical data, assist in diagnostics, and even predict patient outcomes. Machine learning algorithms can process vast amounts of information, enabling healthcare providers to offer more personalized treatments and improve patient care. However, this advancement comes with ethical considerations, such as the reliability of AI in decision-making and the potential for bias in algorithms that could adversely affect certain populations. The dialogue surrounding these issues is essential to ensure that AI serves humanity positively.

Job displacement remains a pressing concern as AI continues to automate tasks traditionally performed by humans. While some industries may experience significant job losses, others are likely to see new opportunities arise. The challenge lies in managing this transition effectively. Upskilling and reskilling the workforce will be vital to preparing individuals for the jobs of the future, many of which will require collaboration with AI systems. It is crucial for policymakers and educational institutions to work together to create pathways that support workers affected by these changes.

Environmental sustainability is another critical area where AI is making a positive impact. AI technologies are being deployed to optimize energy usage, reduce waste, and enhance resource management. For instance, smart grids powered by AI can forecast energy demand and supply, leading to more efficient energy consumption. As climate change becomes an increasingly urgent issue, leveraging AI for environmental solutions can help drive significant progress toward sustainability goals. However, this also invites scrutiny regarding the energy consumption of AI systems themselves, necessitating a balanced approach to development.

The implications of AI extend to personal privacy, as the data-driven nature of many AI applications raises concerns about surveillance and data security. With AI systems collecting and analyzing personal information, the potential for misuse becomes a significant issue that requires robust regulatory frameworks. Balancing innovation with privacy rights is essential to foster public trust in AI technologies. As society navigates these challenges, a collaborative effort among technologists, ethicists, and lawmakers will be essential in shaping a future where AI can be harnessed responsibly and ethically for the benefit of all.

Chapter 2: The Good of AI

Enhancing Efficiency and Productivity

Artificial Intelligence (AI) has emerged as a transformative force across various sectors, significantly enhancing efficiency and productivity. By automating routine tasks and analyzing vast datasets at unprecedented speeds, AI allows organizations to streamline operations and make informed decisions. This evolution is not merely about replacing human labor; rather, it focuses on augmenting human capabilities, enabling workers to focus on higher-value tasks that require creativity and critical thinking. As AI technology continues to evolve, its ability to improve efficiency in both private and public sectors becomes increasingly evident.

In the healthcare sector, AI applications are revolutionizing patient care by optimizing workflows and improving diagnostic accuracy. For instance, AI algorithms can swiftly analyze medical imaging, identifying patterns that might be missed by the human eye. This not only speeds up the diagnostic process but also enhances the precision of treatment plans tailored to individual patients. Consequently, healthcare professionals can allocate more time to direct patient interaction, thereby improving overall care quality while reducing operational burdens on medical facilities.

Education is another area where AI is making significant strides in enhancing productivity. Intelligent tutoring systems can personalize learning experiences, adapting to the unique needs and pace of each student. By automating administrative tasks such as grading and scheduling, educators can devote more time to teaching and mentoring students. Furthermore, AI-driven analytics can provide insights into student performance, helping educators identify at-risk learners and tailor interventions accordingly. This personalized approach not only boosts learning outcomes but also fosters a more engaging educational environment.

AI also plays a crucial role in environmental sustainability efforts. By analyzing environmental data, AI can help organizations optimize resource usage, reduce waste, and improve energy efficiency. For example, smart grids powered by AI technology can manage energy distribution in real time, ensuring that power is used efficiently and reducing the environmental impact of energy consumption. Additionally, predictive analytics can enhance conservation efforts by forecasting ecological changes, enabling proactive measures to protect endangered species and habitats.

While the benefits of AI in enhancing efficiency and productivity are substantial, it is essential to remain vigilant about the ethical implications associated with its use. As organizations increasingly rely on AI technologies, the potential for bias in algorithms and the impact on personal privacy must be addressed. Ensuring transparency and accountability in AI systems is vital to building public trust and safeguarding against unintended consequences. By fostering a dialogue around these issues, society can harness the full potential of AI while mitigating risks, paving the way for a future where technology serves humanity effectively and ethically.

AI in Healthcare Advancements

AI has emerged as a transformative force in healthcare, revolutionizing the way medical professionals diagnose, treat, and manage diseases. Through machine learning algorithms and data analytics, AI systems can analyze vast amounts of patient data, enabling early detection of conditions like cancer and heart disease. These advancements not only enhance the accuracy of diagnoses but also facilitate personalized treatment plans tailored to individual patient needs. As AI becomes more integrated into healthcare, its ability to process and learn from complex datasets will continue to improve, leading to even better health outcomes.

One of the most significant advancements in AI in healthcare is the development of predictive analytics. By leveraging historical patient data, AI can identify patterns and trends that may not be immediately apparent to human clinicians. For instance, predictive models can forecast patient deterioration or the likelihood of hospital readmission, allowing healthcare providers to intervene proactively. This shift from reactive to proactive care not only improves patient safety but also reduces healthcare costs by minimizing unnecessary hospitalizations and treatments.

AI is also playing a crucial role in streamlining administrative workflows within healthcare settings. By automating routine tasks such as scheduling, billing, and patient record management, AI frees up valuable time for healthcare professionals to focus on patient care. This automation enhances operational efficiency and reduces the risk of human error, ultimately leading to a more effective healthcare system. As AI tools continue to evolve, they are expected to further simplify administrative processes, allowing healthcare workers to concentrate on delivering high-quality medical care.

Despite the many benefits, the integration of AI in healthcare raises important ethical considerations. Issues such as data privacy, algorithmic bias, and the potential for job displacement among healthcare workers cannot be overlooked. Ensuring that AI systems are designed and implemented ethically is crucial to maintaining public trust in healthcare technologies. Regulatory frameworks must evolve alongside technological advancements to address these concerns, prioritizing patient safety and equitable access to AI-driven healthcare solutions.

Looking ahead, the future of AI in healthcare holds immense potential. As technology continues to advance, AI could enable groundbreaking developments in areas such as telemedicine, robotic surgery, and drug discovery. However, realizing this potential will require collaboration among healthcare providers, policymakers, and technology developers to create an environment that fosters innovation while safeguarding ethical standards. By navigating the complexities of AI in healthcare, society can harness its benefits while addressing the challenges it presents.

AI in Environmental Sustainability

AI has emerged as a transformative force in the field of environmental sustainability, offering innovative solutions to some of the most pressing ecological challenges of our time. By leveraging vast amounts of data and advanced algorithms, AI can enhance our understanding of environmental systems, optimize resource management, and foster sustainable practices across various industries. From agriculture to energy production, AI technologies are being deployed to minimize waste, reduce emissions, and promote conservation efforts, making them essential tools in the fight against climate change.

In agriculture, AI applications are revolutionizing the way we grow food while minimizing environmental impact. Precision farming techniques powered by AI allow farmers to analyze soil health, monitor crop growth, and manage water usage with remarkable accuracy. By utilizing sensors and satellite imagery, AI systems can provide real-time insights, enabling farmers to make informed decisions about planting, irrigation, and pest control. This not only enhances crop yields but also reduces the overuse of fertilizers and pesticides, leading to healthier ecosystems and less pollution.

The energy sector is another area where AI is making significant strides. Smart grids integrated with AI can optimize energy distribution and consumption patterns, ensuring that renewable energy sources like solar and wind are utilized effectively. By predicting energy demand and identifying inefficiencies, AI can help reduce reliance on fossil fuels and lower greenhouse gas emissions. Moreover, AI-driven technologies are being used to enhance energy storage solutions, making renewable energy more reliable and accessible.

AI's role in environmental monitoring is critical for conservation efforts. Machine learning algorithms can analyze data from various sources, including satellite imagery and sensor networks, to track changes in ecosystems, wildlife populations, and climate patterns. This information is vital for informing policy decisions and conservation

10

strategies. By identifying at-risk species and habitats, AI tools can support targeted interventions, ensuring that resources are allocated efficiently to protect biodiversity and promote ecosystem health.

Despite the promise of AI in promoting environmental sustainability, it is essential to approach its implementation with caution. Ethical considerations, such as the potential for biased algorithms and unequal access to technology, must be addressed to ensure that AI solutions do not inadvertently exacerbate existing inequalities. As we harness AI's capabilities for environmental stewardship, a collaborative effort between technologists, policymakers, and communities is necessary to create frameworks that prioritize equity and sustainability in our pursuit of a greener future.

AI in Education: Enhancing Learning Experiences

AI in education has the potential to revolutionize how learning experiences are structured and delivered. By integrating artificial intelligence into educational frameworks, institutions can provide personalized learning journeys that cater to the unique needs of each student. This customization empowers learners to progress at their own pace, ensuring that they grasp foundational concepts before moving on to more advanced material. AI-driven platforms can assess individual performance in real-time, offering tailored resources and interventions that enhance understanding and retention.

Adaptive learning technologies, powered by AI, are at the forefront of this transformation. These systems analyze data from student interactions to identify strengths and weaknesses, allowing educators to modify their teaching strategies accordingly. For instance, if a student struggles with a specific math concept, the AI can recommend targeted exercises or supplementary materials that focus on that area. This not only supports the student's learning but also alleviates some of the burdens on teachers, who can direct their attention to those who need it most.

Furthermore, AI can facilitate collaborative learning experiences that transcend geographical barriers. Through intelligent tutoring systems and virtual classrooms, students from different parts of the world can engage in meaningful discussions and group projects. This fosters a global learning community where diverse perspectives enrich the educational process. Additionally, AI can help in matching students with peers who have complementary skills, promoting teamwork and mutual learning.

The use of AI in education also raises important ethical considerations. While the technology offers significant benefits, it is crucial to ensure that it is implemented fairly and equitably. Issues such as data privacy, algorithmic bias, and accessibility must be addressed to prevent exacerbating existing inequalities. Educational institutions must prioritize transparency in the use of AI tools, ensuring that both students and educators understand how data is collected and utilized to inform learning processes.

Looking to the future, the role of AI in education is likely to expand further, with innovations that enhance both teaching and learning. As AI continues to evolve, it will open new avenues for creative expression and critical thinking, equipping students with the skills they need for a rapidly changing world. By embracing these advancements while remaining vigilant about their implications, society can harness the power of AI to create more effective and inclusive educational experiences for all learners.

Chapter 3: The Bad of AI

Job Displacement: Opportunities and Challenges

Job displacement due to artificial intelligence (AI) has emerged as a pressing issue in contemporary society, presenting both significant opportunities and challenges. As AI technologies evolve and become integrated into various sectors, the workforce faces a paradigm shift. Routine tasks that were once performed by humans are increasingly being handled by intelligent machines, prompting concerns about job security and the future of work. While the fear of widespread unemployment is valid, it is essential to approach this topic with a nuanced understanding of the potential benefits that AI can bring to the labor market.

One of the primary opportunities arising from AI-related job displacement is the potential for job creation in new fields. As AI automates repetitive tasks, it paves the way for the development of entirely new industries and roles that did not previously exist. For example, the rise of AI technology has led to increased demand for data scientists, AI ethicists, and machine learning engineers. These positions require specialized skills, which can lead to higher wages and improved job satisfaction. Furthermore, as businesses adopt AI to enhance their operations, there is an opportunity for workers to transition into roles that leverage human creativity, emotional intelligence, and complex problem-solving abilities—qualities that machines currently struggle to replicate.

However, the transition to an AI-driven economy is fraught with challenges, particularly regarding workforce retraining and reskilling. Many workers in traditional industries may find themselves ill-equipped to navigate this new landscape. The speed of technological advancement often outpaces the education system's ability to adapt, leaving a skills gap that can result in increased unemployment and economic inequality. To mitigate these challenges, it is crucial for both governments and private sectors to invest in comprehensive retraining programs that equip workers with the necessary skills to thrive in an AI-enhanced environment. This requires a collaborative effort to ensure that education and training initiatives align with the demands of the evolving job market.

Moreover, job displacement raises ethical implications that society must address. The socioeconomic divide could widen if certain populations are unable to access the resources needed to adapt to technological changes. Vulnerable groups, including low-income workers and those in less-skilled jobs, may face greater challenges in finding new employment opportunities. Policymakers must consider equitable strategies that promote inclusivity and provide support for those adversely affected by AI. This may include implementing safety nets, such as universal basic income or enhanced unemployment benefits, to cushion the impact of job loss while facilitating transitions into new roles.

In conclusion, job displacement due to AI presents a complex interplay of opportunities and challenges that demand careful consideration. While the potential for new job creation and enhanced roles exists, the risks associated with workforce displacement and ethical implications cannot be overlooked. As society navigates this transition, it must prioritize education and training, equitable policies, and support systems to ensure that AI serves as a tool for advancement rather than a source of division. Embracing the potential of AI while addressing its challenges will be crucial for fostering a future where technology and humanity coexist harmoniously.

The Impact of AI on Personal Privacy

The integration of artificial intelligence into daily life has transformed the way personal data is collected, analyzed, and utilized. As AI systems become increasingly sophisticated, they can process vast amounts of information to predict behaviors and preferences. This capability, while beneficial in many contexts, raises significant concerns about personal privacy. Users often find themselves unwittingly surrendering their data to algorithms that may not always prioritize their privacy or security. Understanding the implications of AI on personal privacy is essential as society navigates the balance between technological advancement and individual rights.

One of the most pressing issues related to AI and personal privacy is the sheer volume of data collected by various platforms. From social media interactions to online purchases, AI systems aggregate data points that create comprehensive profiles of individuals. These profiles can be used for targeted advertising, personalized content, and even surveillance. The capability of AI to synthesize this information raises questions about consent and the extent to which individuals are aware of how their data is being used. Many people engage with technology without fully understanding the trade-offs involved, leading to a sense of vulnerability regarding their personal information.

Moreover, the potential for data breaches and misuse is heightened in an AI-driven environment. Organizations that leverage AI often store sensitive data to improve their services, but this also makes them attractive targets for cybercriminals. High-profile data breaches have demonstrated that even well-established companies are not immune to attacks. When personal data is compromised, the repercussions can be severe, affecting individuals' financial security and personal safety. This vulnerability creates a need for robust regulatory frameworks to protect consumers and enforce accountability for organizations that handle personal data.

In addition to the risk of data breaches, there is also the issue of surveillance through AI technologies. Governments and corporations can utilize AI to monitor individuals' activities, often under the guise of security or improved service delivery. Such surveillance can lead to a chilling effect on personal freedoms, where individuals alter their behavior due to the awareness of being watched. This dynamic underscores the importance of creating ethical guidelines that govern the use of AI in monitoring and surveillance contexts, ensuring that individual privacy is respected while still addressing legitimate safety concerns.

Finally, the future of AI and personal privacy will likely hinge on public awareness and advocacy. As individuals become more informed about their digital footprints and the implications of AI technologies, there may be increased demand for transparency and control over personal data. Engaging in discussions about ethical AI practices and advocating for stronger privacy protections will be crucial in shaping a future where technology enhances lives without compromising individual rights. The ongoing conversation surrounding AI and personal privacy will play a pivotal role in determining how society balances innovation with the fundamental need for privacy.

Bias in AI Algorithms: Causes and Solutions

Bias in AI algorithms is a critical issue that stems from various sources, fundamentally linked to the data used to train these systems. Machine learning models learn patterns from historical data, which often reflects societal biases. For instance, if a dataset contains biased information, the AI will likely replicate those biases in its predictions or decisions. This can manifest in numerous ways, such as racial or gender discrimination in hiring processes or unequal access to healthcare resources. Understanding the root causes of bias is essential for addressing its implications and ensuring that AI systems promote fairness and equality.

One of the primary causes of bias in AI algorithms is the lack of diversity in training data. When datasets predominantly feature certain demographics or perspectives, the resulting models may overlook or misrepresent others. For example, facial recognition systems trained on images of predominantly white individuals may perform poorly on people of color. Additionally, the way data is collected can introduce bias; for instance, survey methodologies that favor certain populations can skew results. Recognizing these shortcomings in data collection and representation is the first step toward mitigating bias in AI.

Another significant factor contributing to bias is the design of the algorithms themselves. Developers may unconsciously embed their own biases into the algorithms, influenced by their backgrounds and experiences. Moreover, the processes that govern the selection of features within a model can favor certain traits over others, leading to skewed outcomes. The complexity of machine learning models also complicates the detection of bias, as the workings of these systems can be opaque. Addressing these algorithmic biases requires a concerted effort from developers to implement more equitable design practices and to remain vigilant about the potential for bias in their decision-making processes.

Solutions to combat bias in AI algorithms involve a multifaceted approach that includes improving data diversity, enhancing algorithm transparency, and fostering interdisciplinary collaboration. Increasing the variety of datasets used for training can lead to more representative models, while transparency in how algorithms function can help stakeholders identify and rectify biases. Furthermore, involving ethicists, sociologists, and diverse communities in the development process can provide valuable insights that may otherwise be overlooked. This collaborative effort can create a more inclusive framework for AI that prioritizes fairness and accountability.

Ultimately, the responsibility for addressing bias in AI algorithms lies not only with developers and researchers but also with policymakers and society at large. Establishing regulatory frameworks that promote ethical AI development and usage is essential for mitigating bias and ensuring responsible AI deployment. Public awareness and engagement are crucial in holding organizations accountable for their AI practices. By fostering a culture of ethical AI development, society can harness the benefits of artificial intelligence while minimizing its risks, thereby paving the way for a future where AI serves the greater good.

Chapter 4: Ethical Implications of AI in Society

Defining Ethics in AI

Defining ethics in artificial intelligence involves understanding the principles that guide the development and deployment of AI technologies. At its core, ethics in AI seeks to ensure that these systems are designed and operated in ways that are beneficial to society while minimizing harm. This includes considerations of fairness, accountability, transparency, and respect for individual rights. As AI becomes increasingly integrated into various aspects of daily life, from healthcare to education, the ethical implications of its use will play a critical role in shaping public perception and trust in these technologies.

One of the most pressing ethical concerns is the potential for bias in AI algorithms. These biases often stem from the data used to train AI systems, which can reflect societal prejudices or historical inequalities. When AI is deployed in sensitive areas such as hiring, law enforcement, or loan approvals, biased algorithms can perpetuate discrimination and inequality. Addressing this issue requires a concerted effort to develop strategies for identifying, mitigating, and eliminating biases in AI models, ensuring that they operate fairly across diverse populations.

Transparency is another crucial aspect of ethical AI. Users and affected individuals should have a clear understanding of how AI systems make decisions, particularly in high-stakes scenarios like healthcare diagnostics or criminal justice. Ethical AI development emphasizes the need for explainability, where AI systems can provide insights into their decision-making processes. This transparency fosters trust and allows users to challenge or appeal decisions made by AI, promoting accountability among developers and organizations that deploy these technologies.

The ethical implications of AI also extend to personal privacy. As AI systems often rely on vast amounts of data, including personal information, there is a risk of infringing on individual privacy rights. Ethical frameworks must address how data is collected, stored, and used, ensuring that individuals have control over their information and that their privacy is respected. Striking a balance between leveraging data for innovation and protecting individual privacy is essential for the responsible advancement of AI.

Finally, the ethical considerations surrounding AI must be integrated into regulatory frameworks that govern its development and use. Policymakers, technologists, and ethicists must collaborate to create guidelines that not only promote innovation but also safeguard public interests. These frameworks should address issues such as accountability for AI actions, the ethical use of AI in national security, and the implications of AI on job displacement. By fostering a dialogue on ethical AI, society can navigate the complexities of this technology and work towards a future where AI serves the common good.

Responsibility and Accountability in AI Development

Responsibility and accountability in AI development are crucial components that impact various facets of society. As artificial intelligence continues to evolve and integrate into our daily lives, the implications of its use must be carefully considered. Developers and organizations behind AI technologies hold a significant responsibility to ensure that their creations are ethical, transparent, and beneficial for all. This responsibility extends beyond mere compliance with regulations; it encompasses a moral obligation to consider the broader societal impacts of their work.

One major aspect of responsibility in AI development is the need for transparency. Users of AI systems, whether in healthcare, education, or other sectors, should have a clear understanding of how these systems operate and make decisions. This transparency fosters trust between developers and users, ensuring that individuals are informed about the capabilities and limitations of AI systems. When people understand how AI works, they are better equipped to navigate its complexities, thereby reducing the likelihood of misuse or misunderstanding.

Accountability is another essential element in the AI landscape. As AI systems are increasingly involved in critical decision-making processes, the question of who is responsible for the outcomes of those decisions becomes paramount. Developers, organizations, and policymakers must establish clear lines of accountability to address any negative consequences that may arise from AI usage. This includes creating mechanisms for redress when AI systems cause harm, whether through biased decision-making, privacy violations, or other failures. Without accountability, the risks associated with AI could lead to significant societal harm.

The ethical implications of AI also highlight the importance of responsibility and accountability. Developers must actively engage with ethical considerations, such as bias in algorithms and the potential for job displacement. By prioritizing fairness and inclusivity in their designs, AI developers can mitigate the risk of exacerbating existing inequalities. Additionally, fostering a diverse team of stakeholders in the development process can aid in identifying potential biases and ensuring that the technology serves a wide range of communities fairly.

In conclusion, as AI continues to advance and permeate various sectors, the concepts of responsibility and accountability must remain at the forefront of development discussions. By embracing transparency, establishing accountability measures, and engaging with ethical implications, developers can create AI systems that not only enhance efficiency but also promote social good. This proactive approach will help ensure that AI's integration into society supports positive outcomes, ultimately shaping a future where technology serves humanity effectively and equitably.

The Role of Transparency in AI Systems

Transparency in AI systems is essential for fostering trust and understanding among users and stakeholders. As artificial intelligence increasingly permeates various aspects of daily life, from healthcare to education and even national security, the demand for transparency becomes more pronounced. When individuals and organizations understand how AI systems operate, they can engage with these technologies more confidently, ensuring that they are used effectively and ethically. Transparency involves not only clarifying how decisions are made by AI but also making the underlying data and algorithms accessible and understandable to users.

One of the key benefits of transparency in AI is the mitigation of bias. AI systems often learn from historical data, which can include inherent biases reflecting societal inequalities. By being transparent about how data is processed and used, developers can identify potential biases in algorithms and address them proactively. This not only improves the fairness of AI outcomes but also helps build public confidence that AI technologies are designed with ethical considerations in mind. A transparent approach encourages a collaborative dialogue between developers, users, and affected communities to ensure that AI serves the broader interests of society.

In sectors like healthcare, transparency in AI applications can significantly impact patient outcomes. AI-driven tools that assist in diagnostics or treatment recommendations must be understandable to both healthcare providers and patients. When medical professionals can interpret how an AI system arrives at a specific recommendation, they can make more informed decisions in collaboration with the technology. This synergy between human expertise and AI capabilities is crucial for enhancing the quality of care, as well as ensuring that patients feel empowered and informed about their treatment options.

Transparency also plays a critical role in addressing concerns about privacy. As AI systems often rely on vast amounts of personal data to function effectively, users need to know how their information is collected, stored, and used. Clear communication about data handling practices can help alleviate fears of misuse or unauthorized access, fostering a sense of security among users. Establishing trust through transparency not only benefits individuals but also enhances the reputation of organizations that deploy AI technologies, setting a standard for responsible AI usage in society.

Finally, the creation of regulatory frameworks for AI development and use hinges on transparency. Policymakers require clear insights into how AI systems operate to establish guidelines that safeguard public interests. By promoting transparency, stakeholders can engage in informed discussions about the ethical implications of AI, guiding the creation of laws that protect individuals while encouraging innovation. A transparent approach to AI not only empowers users and fosters trust but also paves the way for responsible governance, ensuring that AI technologies contribute positively to society's future.

Chapter 5: The Future of AI

AI in Creative Industries

The integration of artificial intelligence into creative industries has transformed the landscape of art, music, film, and literature in unprecedented ways. AI technologies are increasingly being utilized as tools for artists, writers, and musicians, enabling them to explore new possibilities and expand their creative horizons. From algorithm-generated artwork to AI-assisted music composition, the capabilities of AI are pushing the boundaries of human creativity. This evolution raises important questions about the nature of creativity itself and the role that machines can play in artistic expression.

One of the most notable applications of AI in creative industries is in the realm of visual arts. AI algorithms can analyze vast datasets of existing artworks, learning styles and techniques that can be replicated or innovated upon. Tools like DeepArt and DALL-E enable users to create stunning images based on specific input parameters, effectively blending human intention with machine capabilities. This collaboration between artists and AI not only fosters new artistic expressions but also prompts discussions about authorship and originality, as the lines between human and machine-generated art blur.

In the music industry, AI is making significant strides by assisting composers and producers in creating new sounds and melodies. Platforms like Amper Music and AIVA utilize machine learning to generate compositions that can fit various genres and moods, offering musicians a new palette of sounds to work with. While some fear that AI-generated music may diminish the value of human creativity, others argue that it serves as a catalyst for innovation, allowing artists to experiment and push their creative limits. This duality highlights the ongoing debate about the importance of human touch versus technological enhancement in creative processes.

The film industry is also embracing AI technology, particularly in areas such as scriptwriting, editing, and even acting. AI algorithms can analyze audience preferences and predict successful plotlines or character arcs, providing valuable insights for filmmakers. Additionally, AI-driven tools can streamline editing processes, making them more efficient and less time-consuming. However, the reliance on AI to dictate creative decisions raises ethical concerns regarding artistic integrity and the potential homogenization of content, as studios may prioritize algorithmically favored narratives over unique or unconventional stories.

As AI continues to influence creative industries, it is crucial for stakeholders to navigate the ethical implications and potential challenges it presents. Ensuring that AI serves as a complement to human creativity rather than a replacement is essential to maintaining the richness of artistic expression. Furthermore, discussions around intellectual property rights, the definition of creativity, and the potential for job displacement in creative roles must be addressed. By fostering a collaborative relationship between AI and human creators, the creative industries can harness the benefits of technology while preserving the essence of what makes art and creativity uniquely human.

AI in National Security and Defense

AI's integration into national security and defense represents a transformative shift in how nations protect their interests and respond to threats. With capabilities ranging from data analysis to autonomous systems, AI enhances situational awareness and decision-making processes. By analyzing vast amounts of data from satellite imagery, social media, and intelligence reports, AI can identify potential threats more swiftly and accurately than traditional methods. This capability allows defense agencies to allocate resources more effectively and respond to crises in real-time, potentially saving lives and preventing conflicts.

The application of AI in military operations extends beyond surveillance and intelligence gathering. It includes the development of autonomous weapons systems, which can make decisions on targeting without human intervention. While these technologies promise increased efficiency, they also raise significant ethical concerns. The possibility of machines making life-and-death decisions without human oversight challenges fundamental principles of accountability and morality in warfare. The debate over the use of AI in combat emphasizes the need for robust ethical guidelines and international agreements to govern these technologies.

Furthermore, AI's role in cyber defense is crucial as nations face increasing threats from cyberattacks. AI systems can detect and respond to potential breaches in real-time, analyzing patterns and anomalies that human operators might miss. This proactive defense mechanism is vital for protecting critical infrastructure and sensitive information from adversaries. However, as AI becomes a tool for defense, it also attracts the attention of malicious actors who may seek to exploit these technologies, leading to an ongoing arms race in the cyber domain.

The implications of AI in national security extend to the socio-political landscape as well. Governments must navigate the balance between enhancing security and preserving civil liberties. The deployment of AI surveillance technologies can lead to privacy invasions and disproportionate monitoring of certain communities. As nations adopt these advanced technologies, it is essential to establish transparent policies that ensure accountability and protect individual rights, fostering public trust while maintaining security.

In conclusion, the future of AI in national security and defense is a double-edged sword. While it offers innovative solutions for identifying and neutralizing threats, it also presents challenges that require careful consideration of ethical implications and regulatory frameworks. As society grapples with the consequences of AI, it is vital to engage in an ongoing dialogue about the responsible use of these technologies, ensuring they serve the common good without compromising fundamental human values.

Emerging Technologies and AI Integration

Emerging technologies are continuously reshaping the landscape of artificial intelligence, driving innovation and offering new opportunities across various sectors. As AI systems become more advanced, their integration into everyday processes and industries is accelerating. This convergence of emerging technologies such as machine learning, natural language processing, blockchain, and the Internet of Things (IoT) is creating a robust framework that enhances the capabilities of AI, making it more effective in solving complex problems. These developments hold the promise of improving productivity, streamlining operations, and creating new avenues for growth in both established and emerging sectors.

One of the notable impacts of AI integration is evident in healthcare advancements. The combination of AI and emerging technologies allows for more accurate diagnoses, personalized treatment plans, and predictive analytics that can foresee patient needs. For example, AI algorithms can analyze vast amounts of medical data to identify patterns that may not be apparent to human practitioners. This capability not only enhances the quality of care but also optimizes resource allocation within healthcare systems, which is crucial as demand increases globally. The ethical implications of these technologies must also be considered, particularly regarding patient privacy and the potential for algorithmic bias in treatment recommendations.

In the realm of environmental sustainability, AI is playing a transformative role. Advanced algorithms can analyze environmental data to predict climate patterns, optimize energy consumption, and enhance resource management. By integrating AI with emerging technologies such as drones and sensor networks, organizations can monitor ecosystems more effectively and respond to environmental changes in real-time. This synergy not only helps in conservation efforts but also supports businesses in adopting sustainable practices, which are increasingly demanded by consumers and regulatory bodies alike.

The integration of AI into education presents another significant opportunity. Emerging technologies facilitate personalized learning experiences that cater to individual student needs and learning styles. AI-driven platforms can assess student performance and provide tailored resources, making education more accessible and effective. However, the implementation of these technologies raises questions about equity, as disparities in access to technology can exacerbate existing educational inequalities. Addressing these issues will be crucial to ensure that the benefits of AI in education are equitably distributed.

Lastly, the future of AI in creative industries is beginning to take shape with the integration of emerging technologies. AI systems are now capable of generating music, art, and literature, challenging traditional notions of creativity. While this raises exciting possibilities, it also prompts discussions about authorship, originality, and the role of human creativity in an increasingly automated world. As these technologies evolve, society must navigate the balance between celebrating innovation and preserving the intrinsic value of human expression, ensuring that the integration of AI contributes positively to our cultural landscape.

Chapter 6: Regulatory Frameworks for AI Development and Use

Current Regulations and Guidelines

Current regulations and guidelines surrounding artificial intelligence (AI) are increasingly critical as the technology continues to evolve and permeate various aspects of society. Governments and regulatory bodies are working to establish frameworks that address ethical implications, ensure safety, and promote responsible use of AI. The rapid development of AI technologies has outpaced the creation of comprehensive legal structures, prompting a need for urgent attention to how these guidelines can effectively mitigate risks while fostering innovation.

In many regions, regulations focus on data protection and privacy, recognizing that AI systems often rely on vast amounts of personal data. The General Data Protection Regulation (GDPR) in the European Union serves as a leading example, mandating transparency in data usage, consent from individuals, and the right to be forgotten. Such regulations are crucial in addressing concerns about surveillance and personal privacy, as they compel organizations to prioritize ethical data handling practices. As AI becomes more integrated into everyday life, similar frameworks are emerging globally to protect individuals from potential abuses.

Another significant area of focus is the impact of AI on employment and job displacement. Various guidelines are being proposed to ensure that the workforce is prepared for the changes brought about by automation. This includes initiatives aimed at reskilling workers and promoting educational programs that emphasize digital literacy and adaptability. Policymakers are beginning to recognize the importance of balancing technological advancement with the need for economic stability, leading to discussions about universal basic income and other social safety nets as potential solutions to workforce disruptions.

AI's role in healthcare and environmental sustainability is also under scrutiny, with regulations emerging to ensure that these technologies are used responsibly. In healthcare, guidelines are being developed to maintain patient confidentiality while encouraging the use of AI for diagnostics and treatment planning. Concurrently, in environmental contexts, regulations are focusing on the sustainable use of AI to address climate change and resource management effectively. These regulations aim to harness AI's potential for positive societal impacts while preventing misuse or unintended consequences.

Finally, the issue of bias in AI algorithms has gained significant attention, prompting calls for regulations that promote fairness and accountability. Guidelines are being established to ensure that AI systems are developed with diverse datasets and undergo rigorous testing to minimize bias. This is vital in areas such as criminal justice, hiring practices, and loan approvals, where biased algorithms can perpetuate existing inequalities. Ongoing dialogue among technologists, ethicists, and policymakers is essential to create a regulatory landscape that addresses these challenges while encouraging the ethical advancement of AI technologies.

Challenges in Regulating AI

The rapid advancement of artificial intelligence technologies presents a myriad of challenges in the realm of regulation. As AI systems become more integrated into various aspects of society, from healthcare to education, the need for effective regulatory frameworks becomes increasingly critical. One of the primary challenges is the pace at which AI evolves. Regulators often struggle to keep up with technological advancements, leading to gaps in oversight that can result in unintended consequences. This lag can exacerbate ethical dilemmas and complicate the task of ensuring that AI is used for the benefit of society while minimizing harm.

Another significant challenge in regulating AI is the complexity and opacity of many AI systems. Machine learning models, particularly deep learning algorithms, can behave in unpredictable ways, making it difficult for regulators to understand how decisions are made. This lack of transparency raises concerns about accountability, especially in high-stakes areas such as healthcare and criminal justice. As these systems become more autonomous, the question of who is responsible for their actions becomes increasingly complicated, complicating efforts to establish clear regulatory guidelines.

Bias in AI algorithms presents an additional hurdle for regulators. AI systems can inadvertently perpetuate or even amplify existing societal biases if they are trained on flawed data sets. This issue is particularly concerning in applications related to hiring, lending, and law enforcement, where biased algorithms can lead to discrimination and exacerbate existing inequalities. Addressing these biases requires not only technical solutions but also a comprehensive understanding of the social contexts in which AI operates. Regulators must work collaboratively with AI developers, ethicists, and affected communities to create standards that promote fairness and equity.

The global nature of AI development adds another layer of complexity to regulation. Different countries have varying approaches to AI governance, and the lack of a unified international framework can create challenges in enforcing standards. This disparity can lead to a regulatory race to the bottom, where companies relocate to jurisdictions with lenient regulations, undermining efforts to ensure ethical AI practices. As AI technologies cross borders, it becomes imperative for nations to cooperate and establish shared principles that prioritize safety, ethics, and human rights.

Lastly, the potential for AI to impact employment raises critical questions about the future of work and the economy. As AI systems automate tasks traditionally performed by humans, there is a pressing need for regulators to address the implications for job displacement and workforce development. This involves not only creating policies that support workers affected by automation but also investing in education and retraining programs to prepare the workforce for an AI-driven economy. Balancing innovation with social responsibility will be essential in fostering an environment where AI can thrive while ensuring that societal values are upheld.

The Role of International Cooperation in AI Regulation

The rapidly evolving landscape of artificial intelligence (AI) presents both unique opportunities and substantial challenges, underscoring the need for international cooperation in the regulation of AI technologies. As AI systems increasingly transcend national boundaries, the implications of their use and development affect multiple countries and cultures. International cooperation can facilitate the establishment of universal standards and guidelines that ensure the ethical deployment of AI while promoting innovation. By coordinating efforts among nations, the global community can work towards shared objectives, such as enhancing public safety, ensuring fairness, and protecting individual rights.

A collaborative approach to AI regulation can help mitigate the risks of technological disparities among nations. Countries with advanced AI capabilities may inadvertently dominate the landscape, leading to power imbalances and inequities in access to AI benefits. Through international partnerships, nations can share knowledge, resources, and best practices, enabling less technologically advanced countries to enhance their AI capabilities responsibly. This would not only promote equity but also foster a more inclusive global economy where all nations can participate in AI-driven growth.

Furthermore, international cooperation is essential in addressing the ethical implications of AI deployment. Issues such as bias in algorithms, privacy concerns, and the potential for job displacement require a collective effort to develop ethical frameworks that guide AI development. By engaging in dialogue and collaboration, countries can share insights and experiences that contribute to the creation of ethical guidelines that consider diverse cultural values and perspectives. This collaborative dialogue can also help identify shared ethical principles that can serve as a foundation for responsible AI use worldwide.

The role of international cooperation also extends to ensuring compliance with regulations and monitoring AI developments. As AI technology evolves rapidly, the regulatory landscape must adapt accordingly. International partnerships can facilitate the sharing of regulatory practices and success stories, helping countries to build robust regulatory frameworks suited to their specific contexts. By working together, nations can develop mechanisms for monitoring AI applications, ensuring accountability, and addressing transnational challenges like cybersecurity threats or the misuse of AI in surveillance.

Lastly, fostering international cooperation in AI regulation can enhance public trust in technology. As concerns about AI's impact on society grow, transparent and collaborative regulatory efforts can reassure the public that their interests are being prioritized. By demonstrating a commitment to ethical AI development and responsible governance, nations can build confidence among citizens, encouraging a more positive perception of AI technologies. This trust is vital for ensuring that AI can be harnessed as a force for good, addressing societal challenges while enabling advancements across various sectors, including healthcare, education, and environmental sustainability.

Chapter 7: Navigating the AI Landscape

Strategies for Individuals and Organizations

The rapid evolution of artificial intelligence (AI) presents both opportunities and challenges for individuals and organizations. To navigate this complex landscape, it is essential to implement effective strategies tailored to the specific needs and contexts of users. Individuals can begin by fostering a growth mindset that embraces lifelong learning. This approach will enable them to adapt to the changing job market and acquire new skills that complement AI technologies. Engaging in online courses, workshops, and community discussions can enhance understanding and proficiency in AI, ultimately empowering individuals to leverage these tools effectively in their careers.

Organizations, on the other hand, should prioritize the development of ethical AI frameworks. Establishing clear guidelines that address ethical implications, such as bias in algorithms and the protection of personal privacy, is crucial for responsible AI implementation. By creating diverse teams that include ethicists, data scientists, and industry experts, organizations can ensure that AI systems are designed with fairness and transparency in mind. This collaborative approach not only mitigates risks but also fosters trust among stakeholders, enhancing the organization's reputation and commitment to ethical practices.

Moreover, both individuals and organizations must actively participate in advocacy for robust regulatory frameworks governing AI development and use. Engaging with policymakers and industry leaders can help shape regulations that promote innovation while safeguarding public interests. Individuals can lend their voices to discussions around AI ethics and governance, ensuring that diverse perspectives are considered. Organizations can contribute by sharing best practices and case studies that highlight the benefits and challenges of AI implementation, thereby influencing policies that support sustainable and equitable AI advancements.

In the context of job displacement, proactive strategies are necessary for individuals and organizations alike. Individuals should focus on reskilling and upskilling to remain competitive in a labor market increasingly influenced by AI. Organizations can play a pivotal role by investing in training programs that prepare employees for new roles created by AI technologies. By fostering a culture of adaptability and continuous learning, both parties can harness the potential of AI while mitigating the risks of job loss.

Lastly, the role of AI in enhancing sectors such as healthcare, education, and environmental sustainability cannot be overlooked. Individuals should seek to understand how AI tools can improve their personal and professional lives, while organizations must explore innovative applications of AI that address societal challenges. Collaborating with researchers and industry experts can lead to breakthroughs in areas like personalized medicine, educational technologies, and sustainable practices. By embracing AI responsibly, individuals and organizations can contribute to a future where technology serves as a catalyst for positive change in society.

Future Trends in AI Technology

The future of AI technology is poised to bring profound changes across multiple sectors, reflecting a blend of innovation and ethical considerations. As AI systems become increasingly sophisticated, their applications are expected to expand far beyond current capabilities. One of the most significant trends is the integration of AI with other emerging technologies, such as quantum computing and advanced robotics. This convergence could lead to unprecedented computational power and problem-solving abilities, enabling breakthroughs in areas like drug discovery and climate modeling. However, this also necessitates a critical examination of the ethical frameworks guiding such advancements, ensuring that they benefit society as a whole.

In the realm of employment, AI's impact is likely to be dual-faceted. While automation may displace certain jobs, it is also expected to create new opportunities in fields requiring human insight and creativity. A shift towards more AI-driven workplaces could necessitate a reevaluation of workforce skills, with an emphasis on adaptability and continuous learning. Educational institutions and businesses will need to collaborate to develop training programs that equip individuals with the skills required to thrive in this evolving landscape. As AI continues to evolve, the dialogue surrounding job displacement must also consider the potential for enhanced productivity and the creation of entirely new job categories.

Healthcare is another area where AI is set to make significant strides. The future of AI technology in this field includes advancements in personalized medicine, where algorithms analyze genetic information alongside lifestyle factors to tailor treatments to individual patients. Furthermore, AI-driven diagnostic tools are expected to improve accuracy and speed, potentially leading to earlier detection of diseases. As these technologies advance, ethical implications surrounding patient privacy and data security will need to be addressed, ensuring that trust in healthcare systems is maintained while harnessing the benefits of AI.

Environmental sustainability is increasingly becoming a focal point for AI research and application. Future trends include the use of AI for more efficient resource management, such as optimizing energy consumption in smart grids or enhancing precision agriculture to reduce waste. These innovations can contribute to significant environmental benefits, helping to combat climate change and promote sustainable practices. However, the deployment of AI technologies in this context must be approached with caution, as the environmental impact of developing and maintaining AI systems themselves also warrants consideration.

The regulatory landscape surrounding AI is likely to evolve in response to these advancements and their societal implications. Governments and organizations around the world are beginning to recognize the need for comprehensive frameworks that address the ethical, legal, and social challenges posed by AI. These frameworks will play a crucial role in ensuring that AI technologies are developed and implemented responsibly, balancing innovation with accountability. As AI continues to shape various aspects of society, ongoing discussions about its regulation will be essential to safeguard public interests while fostering an environment conducive to technological progress.

Preparing for an AI-Driven Society

Preparing for an AI-driven society requires a multifaceted approach that addresses the technological, ethical, and social implications of artificial intelligence. As AI continues to permeate various sectors, from healthcare to education, it is essential for individuals and communities to understand the transformative potential of these technologies. This understanding will enable society to harness AI's benefits while mitigating its risks. Awareness of how AI operates and its implications for daily life lays the foundation for informed decision-making and responsible usage.

The ethical implications of AI are paramount as society integrates these systems into everyday operations. Questions regarding privacy, bias, and accountability must be prioritized. The potential for AI to perpetuate existing biases, especially in hiring practices or law enforcement, necessitates a commitment to developing fair and transparent algorithms. By engaging in discussions about ethical AI practices, individuals can advocate for regulations that ensure technology serves the greater good. Educating the public about these issues will foster a culture of accountability and oversight that aligns with societal values.

Job displacement is another critical concern associated with the rise of AI. While automation can lead to increased efficiency and economic growth, it also poses challenges for the workforce. Preparing for this shift involves proactive measures, such as reskilling and upskilling programs that equip workers with the necessary tools to thrive in an AI-enhanced job market. Emphasizing the need for adaptability and continuous learning will empower individuals to navigate changes in employment landscapes, turning potential threats into opportunities for personal and professional growth.

AI's role in environmental sustainability presents a promising avenue for addressing climate change and resource management challenges. Innovative applications of AI, such as optimizing energy consumption and improving agricultural practices, can significantly contribute to sustainability efforts. Preparing for an AI-driven society includes advocating for the integration of these technologies into environmental policies and practices. By leveraging AI's capabilities, society can work towards a more sustainable future, balancing economic development with ecological preservation.

Finally, preparing for an AI-driven society means fostering an informed public dialogue about the future of AI in various sectors. From healthcare advancements that improve patient outcomes to the ethical considerations surrounding national security applications, a comprehensive understanding of AI's potential is crucial. Encouraging discussions about regulatory frameworks and the responsible use of AI will help shape policies that protect individual rights while promoting innovation. By engaging with these topics, society can collectively navigate the complexities of AI, ensuring that its integration enhances the quality of life for all.

Chapter 8: Conclusion

The Path Forward for AI

The trajectory of artificial intelligence is poised to shape various facets of society in unprecedented ways. As we look ahead, it is critical to embrace a path forward that balances innovation with ethical considerations. This involves fostering an environment where AI technologies can thrive while ensuring that their deployment aligns with societal values and norms. In doing so, we can harness the potential of AI to enhance human capabilities and address pressing global challenges, from healthcare to environmental sustainability.

One of the foremost considerations in advancing AI is the need for robust regulatory frameworks. As AI systems become more integrated into everyday life, it is essential to establish guidelines that govern their development and application. These regulations should focus on transparency, accountability, and fairness to mitigate risks such as bias and discrimination in AI algorithms. By setting clear standards, we can promote trust among users and stakeholders, ensuring that AI serves as a tool for empowerment rather than exclusion.

Job displacement remains a significant concern as AI technologies evolve. However, the narrative surrounding AI and employment should not be solely about loss; it should also encompass the opportunities for new job creation and skill development. As certain roles become automated, there is potential for the emergence of new industries and professions that leverage AI capabilities. Educational systems must adapt to prepare the workforce for these changes, emphasizing lifelong learning and resilience to transition into roles that AI cannot easily replicate.

The role of AI in healthcare is another critical area where the future holds promise. From improving diagnostic accuracy to personalizing treatment plans, AI can revolutionize patient care and outcomes. However, ethical implications surrounding data privacy and consent must be prioritized to protect individuals' rights. Striking a balance between technological advancement and patient autonomy will be essential to foster public trust and encourage the adoption of AI-driven solutions in health services.

Finally, as we envision the future of AI, we must also consider its impact on personal privacy and security. With the increasing reliance on AI systems, safeguarding sensitive information becomes paramount. Collaborative efforts between governments, private sector entities, and civil society are necessary to develop comprehensive strategies that protect individuals while promoting innovation. By prioritizing ethical considerations and societal well-being, we can navigate the complexities of AI and ensure that its benefits are accessible to all, paving the way for a future that harmonizes technological progress with human values.

Balancing Innovation with Ethical Considerations

Balancing innovation with ethical considerations is a crucial endeavor in the rapidly evolving landscape of artificial intelligence. As AI technologies continue to develop at an unprecedented pace, society faces the challenge of harnessing their potential while ensuring that ethical standards guide their implementation. This balance is vital not only for the integrity of technological advancements but also for maintaining public trust in AI systems. Innovations should not only be assessed for their technical capabilities but also for their broader implications on society, culture, and individual rights.

One of the most pressing ethical considerations involves the impact of AI on job displacement. The automation of tasks traditionally performed by humans raises concerns about unemployment and economic inequality. While AI can enhance productivity and create new opportunities, it is essential to address the potential for job loss in certain sectors. Policymakers and businesses must engage in proactive discussions to develop strategies that support workforce transitions and ensure that the benefits of AI are equitably distributed. This includes investing in education and retraining programs that equip individuals with the skills needed for emerging job markets.

In the realm of healthcare, AI holds great promise for improving patient outcomes and streamlining processes. However, the ethical implications of deploying AI in this sensitive field are significant. Issues such as data privacy, informed consent, and algorithmic bias must be carefully navigated to prevent harm to patients and ensure equitable access to healthcare solutions. Healthcare providers and technologists must collaborate to establish guidelines that prioritize patient welfare and ethical standards in AI-driven healthcare innovations.

Environmental sustainability is another area where the ethical balance of AI innovation is critical. AI technologies can contribute to more efficient resource management and environmental conservation efforts. Nonetheless, the development and deployment of these technologies must consider their environmental footprint and potential unintended consequences. Engaging stakeholders from diverse backgrounds, including environmental scientists, ethicists, and technologists, is essential to create frameworks that guide the ethical use of AI in addressing global environmental challenges.

Finally, the issue of bias in AI algorithms serves as a stark reminder of the ethical responsibilities inherent in technological innovation. AI systems can inadvertently perpetuate existing societal biases if not designed and monitored carefully. Addressing these biases requires a commitment to transparency, accountability, and inclusivity in AI development processes. By fostering a culture of ethical awareness and collaboration among AI developers, researchers, and users, society can work towards mitigating bias and ensuring that AI serves as a tool for positive change rather than a source of division.

Final Thoughts on AI's Impact on Humanity

The impact of artificial intelligence on humanity is a multifaceted subject that elicits a spectrum of opinions and emotions. As we navigate through the complexities of AI technologies, it becomes increasingly clear that their influence can be both beneficial and detrimental. On one hand, AI has the potential to revolutionize various sectors, including healthcare, education, and environmental sustainability, by enhancing efficiency, precision, and accessibility. On the other hand, the ethical implications of these advancements raise significant concerns about job displacement, personal privacy, and the potential for bias in algorithmic decision-making.

In healthcare, for instance, AI systems are improving diagnostic accuracy and personalizing treatment plans, leading to better patient outcomes. The use of AI in analyzing vast datasets can uncover patterns and insights that human practitioners might miss. However, as these technologies become more integrated into healthcare systems, it is imperative to address ethical issues surrounding patient data privacy and consent. Ensuring that AI tools are developed and implemented with a focus on ethical standards will be crucial in maintaining public trust and safeguarding individual rights.

Job displacement is another critical concern that accompanies the rise of AI. While automation may lead to the loss of certain jobs, it can also create new opportunities in emerging sectors. The challenge lies in managing this transition effectively. Upskilling and reskilling the workforce will be essential in preparing individuals for the jobs of the future. As we embrace AI technologies, it is vital to foster a dialogue around the societal implications of these changes, ensuring that workers are not left behind in the wake of innovation.

Moreover, the role of AI in addressing environmental challenges cannot be overlooked. AI-driven solutions are already being employed to monitor climate change, optimize resource use, and reduce waste. These advancements hold promise for achieving sustainability goals and mitigating environmental degradation. However, the deployment of AI must be approached cautiously, considering the potential ecological impacts of the technologies themselves, including energy consumption and resource extraction during production.

Ultimately, as we look to the future of AI, it is essential to establish regulatory frameworks that guide the responsible development and use of these technologies. Policymakers, technologists, and ethicists must collaborate to create guidelines that prioritize human welfare and societal benefits. By addressing the ethical implications, potential biases, and the need for transparency in AI systems, we can harness the positive aspects of AI while minimizing its risks. The journey forward requires a collective commitment to navigating the complexities of AI with an informed and proactive approach, ensuring that its impact on humanity is both constructive and equitable.

www.ingramcontent.com/pod-product-compliance
Lightning Source LLC
LaVergne TN
LVHW071523070326
832902LV00002B/57